ONE FOR THE ROAD

A Play

by Willy Russell

samuelfrench.co.uk

THINKING ABOUT PERFORMING A SHOW?

There are thousands of plays and musicals available to perform from Samuel French right now, and applying for a licence is easier and more affordable than you might think

From classic plays to brand new musicals, from monologues to epic dramas, there are shows for everyone.

Plays and musicals are protected by copyright law, so if you want to perform them, the first thing you'll need is a licence. This simple process helps support the playwright by ensuring they get paid for their work and means that you'll have the documents you need to stage the show in public.

Not all our shows are available to perform all the time, so it's important to check and apply for a licence before you start rehearsals or commit to doing the show.

LEARN MORE & FIND THOUSANDS OF SHOWS

Browse our full range of plays and musicals, and find out more about how to license a show

www.samuelfrench.co.uk/perform

Talk to the friendly experts in our Licensing team for advice on choosing a show and help with licensing

plays@samuelfrench.co.uk   020 7387 9373

Acting Editions

BORN TO PERFORM

Playscripts designed from the ground up to work the way you do in rehearsal, performance and study

---

Larger, clearer text for easier reading

Wider margins for notes

Performance features such as character and props lists, sound and lighting cues, and more

---

+ CHOOSE A SIZE AND STYLE TO SUIT YOU

STANDARD EDITION

Our regular paperback book at our regular size

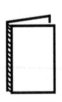

SPIRAL-BOUND EDITION

The same size as the Standard Edition, but with a sturdy, easy-to-fold, easy-to-hold spiral-bound spine

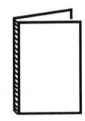

LARGE EDITION

A4 size and spiral bound, with larger text and a blank page for notes opposite every page of text – perfect for technical and directing use

---

LEARN MORE | **samuelfrench.co.uk/actingeditions**

**Other plays by WILLY RUSSELL
published and licensed by Samuel French**

Blood Brothers (musical version)

Breezeblock Park

Educating Rita

I Read the News Today

Our Day Out (A Play with Music)

Shirley Valentine

Stags and Hens

**Other plays by WILLY RUSSELL
licensed by Samuel French**

Blood Brothers (play version)

Boy with the Transistor Radio

Terraces

Our Day Out (musical version)

**FIND PERFECT PLAYS TO PERFORM AT
www.samuelfrench.co.uk/perform**

ABOUT THE AUTHOR

Willy Russell's career spans more than four decades; born in Liverpool in 1947, he left school at fifteen, became a women's hairdresser, part-time singer/songwriter before returning to education and becoming a teacher.

Russell's breakthrough work, commissioned by Liverpool Everyman, *John Paul George Ringo...and Bert* transferred to the West End winning Best Musical - Evening Standard and London Theatre Critics Awards.

Two of Willy's best-known plays have female protagonists, *Educating Rita* (Olivier Award for Best Comedy and *Shirley Valentine* (Olivier Award – Best New Comedy & Best New Actress, Tony Awards, Broadway – Best Actress). Both became successful films - Julie Walters and Pauline Collins who played the roles on stage received Oscar nominations as did Willy Russell for the screenplay of *Educating Rita.*

Blood Brothers, (Laurence Olivier Award, Best New Musical, 1983), played for twenty-four years becoming the third longest running West End musical. Major foreign productions include a two-year run on Broadway, with recent productions in South Africa and Korea and current productions in Australia and Japan. The UK tour is still playing to packed houses.

Our Day Out, originally written for TV, about a school outing, has been adapted for the stage as *Our Day Out - The Musical.* Premiered at Liverpool's Royal Court in 2010 to rave reviews it was revived a year later for another sell-out season.

The critically acclaimed novel, *The Wrong Boy* was published in 2000 and translated worldwide.

For further information please visit willyrussell.com

Photo credit paulcoxphotos.co.uk

ONE FOR THE ROAD

An earlier version of this play was first presented at the Nottingham Playhouse on 7th March 1979, with the following cast of characters:

PAULINE CAIN	Elizabeth Estensen
DENNIS CAIN	Alun Armstrong
ROGER FULLER	Philip Jackson
JANE FULLER	Rachel Davies

Directed by Mike Ockrent
Designed by John Gunter

A revised version of the play, upon which this Acting Edition is based, opened on 4th February 1985 at the Ashcroft Theatre, Croydon, prior to a national tour, presented by Meridian Productions, with the following cast of characters.

DENNIS CAIN	David Cardy
PAULINE CAIN	Ishia Bennison
JANE FULLER	Helen Shapiro
ROGER FULLER	Patrick Monckton

Directed by Deborah Bestwick
Designed by Glenn Willoughby

The action of the play takes place in the lounge of the Cains' dormer bungalow on a modern housing estate in the north of England

ACT I   Early evening
ACT II   Some time later the same evening

Time—the present

ACT I

Before the play begins and as (hopefully) people are beginning to gather, we should hear Joni Mitchell's album, "Blue".

The stage is a lounge in an "executive" dormer bungalow, situated on an estate a few miles from a major northern city. The furnishing is augmented Habitat. The people who live here are "first generation" middle class; their parents still pay rent. Amongst the gadgets and gear there is a dining table and chairs, a video recorder, a stereo unit, a reproduction writing bureau. The set should include a window, with a venetian blind that is pulled up to reveal the back garden, beyond which can be seen row upon row of dormer bungalows stretching into the distance.

As Houselights go down we see **DENNIS** *enter from the hall. He surreptitiously unlocks the drop-down flap of the bureau and puts something inside. He locks the bureau and puts the key into his pocket. He goes to the stereo and sifts through records. He scowls at a John Denver album, snorts at a Manilow record, almost throws up at a Richard Clayderman album then laughs aloud at a second John Denver album. Finally, he finds the Joni Mitchell album, "Blue". He places it carefully on the stereo, sits, and places the headphones on his head. We hear, faintly, the sounds to which he is listening.*

Behind him, unseen and unheard, **PAULINE** *(his wife) enters. She is obviously distraught. She does not see that he has on the headphones. She pulls out a dining chair and sits.*

PAULINE Dennis... I've had enough. From now on...that's it. No more. That's it. I will no longer have our child mixing with those Parnes kids, not when he comes out with words like that. I know he gets it from them. They've got mouths like open sewers, those Parnes kids. Well there's going to be a stop to it. I'm not having it: I'm not having my child telling me that Jack and Jill did not go up the hill for a pail of water but went up for a... Well. You know. It's a disgusting thing for an innocent child to come out with. You're going to have to deal with it Dennis. You're going to have to put a stop to it Dennis. Dennis! Dennis! *(Sensing that she's talking to herself)* Dennis! *(Seeing the situation she goes to the amplifier and plunges up the volume)*

DENNIS *screams and leaps out of his chair, ripping off the headphones.*

You sit there, oblivious, while I'm left to deal with a crisis in the family. Dennis, for God's sake, what's wrong with you?

DENNIS *(in agony)* Me ears...me ears...

PAULINE I'm not talking about that. I'm talking about all this buryin' your head in the sand while I'm left to cope with one calamity after another.

DENNIS So what's wrong now?

PAULINE What's wrong, Dennis, is that we have got a seven-year-old child coming out with obscenities.

DENNIS Like what?

PAULINE John has just informed me that the hill which Jack and Jill climbed was not the scene of collecting water but of...of sexual intercourse.

DENNIS Is that what he said, sexual intercourse?

PAULINE I think you know very well what he said.

DENNIS What?

PAULINE He swore.

DENNIS Well, I realize that, but what did he actually say?

PAULINE He used a word meaning sexual intercourse.

DENNIS Which one?

PAULINE Which one?

DENNIS Yes, which one?

PAULINE If you must know, the worst one.

DENNIS Fuck?

PAULINE Dennis!

DENNIS Well, there's loads of words with that meaning... There's...

PAULINE Well, I dare say there are, but I don't want them spoken in this bungalow.

DENNIS There's shag...

PAULINE DENNIS! *(She grabs the headphones and clamps them over her head)*

DENNIS And root. As in, "I could really root that one".

The following two speeches are spoken simultaneously.

And there's "a leg over", and there's the old fashioned style, "roger", and the more current versions like "shafting" and "balling".

PAULINE I'm not listening, Dennis. I don't know why you want to behave like this. I don't know what's been wrong with you lately but if you ask me I think you should see a doctor.

DENNIS I can't think of anymore. That's about the lot. You can take the cans off now, Pauline. *(He motions to her)*

She turns her back. He goes to the amplifier and plunges up the volume. She screams and rips off the headphones.

PAULINE Shit. You shit!

MUSIC cut off

DENNIS AHA! So now we know where John's been gettin' this filthy language from.

PAULINE Dennis, I'm warnin' you. In matters of this nature I teach John the correct terms, you know I do. I've told you, he's getting this language from those Parnes kids.

DENNIS He doesn't get it from the Parnes kids. If a bomb dropped on this estate the poor bloody Parnes kids'd get the blame.

PAULINE Well if he doesn't get it from them you just tell me where he does pick it up from. I've never heard other children from Phase Two section of the estate who use language like that.

DENNIS Pauline, people swear whether they're on Phase One, Phase Two or Phase Three Thousand and Sixty-Nine. People swear everywhere.

PAULINE They don't Dennis.

DENNIS They do.

PAULINE They don't.

DENNIS They do.

PAULINE Do they? And when was the last time you heard Sue Lawley say "Here's the bleedin' news".

DENNIS I'd forgotten about Sue Lawley.

PAULINE When we moved to Phase Two I thought we'd be gettin' away from all that. Well, that's it, no more. In future John doesn't go out to play in the street. From now on he can just roam the garden.

DENNIS But you can't *roam* a twelve foot lawn.

PAULINE It's not twelve foot. Since we had the greenhouse moved there's a good sixteen foot lawn out there.

DENNIS You can't stop him playin' out. It won't do him any harm.

PAULINE Oh no. It won't harm a seven-year-old if he's subjected to endless obscenities.

DENNIS Of course it won't. Listen, if you want to know, I taught him most of the words myself.

PAULINE *(stunned)* You did what?

DENNIS I had to! I heard him, out in the avenue, tryin' to swear like the rest of them. Poor kid was soundin' like a medical dictionary.

PAULINE Yes. Because I tell John to use only the correct terms. And that's how it should be.

DENNIS But not when you're supposed to be swearin'. It doesn't have quite the same effect.

PAULINE So you'd rather him come out with...with that sort of language?

DENNIS Well, why not?

PAULINE *(disappearing into the kitchen)* All right. All right, if you won't take any notice of me, just wait till your mother gets here. You ask her if you should teach her grandchild the correct terms or the obscenities.

DENNIS I will.

PAULINE Yes, you do.

DENNIS "Now Mother, what do you prefer, cock, or penis?" *(Imitating his mother)* "Well son, if you don't mind, I'd rather just have the mixed salad."

PAULINE *(entering from the kitchen)* Anyway, it won't be long now. Their days are numbered, you mark my words.

DENNIS Whose?

PAULINE You know very well whose. Whoever it is who's responsible for it.

DENNIS For what?

PAULINE Dennis, do you walk around wearing ear-plugs and a blindfold? The whole estate has been up in arms about it for the past month.

DENNIS About what?

PAULINE About the fact that in the last four weeks there have been countless attacks; a dozen garden gnomes have been found with their heads severed. A whole range of fountains and patio waterfalls have been contaminated with Radox; instead of cascading they now do nothing but foam! And what about Shelagh Bennet's Venus de Milo?

DENNIS Well. What about it?

PAULINE It's had arms stuck onto it. Only a warped mind could dream up something like that. What terrifies me is who the next victims will be. We've escaped so far.

DENNIS We have, haven't we?

PAULINE So have Jane and Roger. I should think they have. Who's gonna risk meddling with property belonging to the chair person of the Ladies Karate Club?

DENNIS Ey! Maybe it's them who's doin' it?

PAULINE Dennis, don't be stupid, Jane and Roger are the backbone of Phase Two.

DENNIS But she's always out joggin' isn't she?

PAULINE What's that got to do with it?

DENNIS Everythin'. She's joggin' along late at night, right? No one pays any attention, it's just Jane joggin'. But as she jogs up to some gnome infested garden, she leaps over the wall, pulls a lump hammer from out of her track suit and wallop, wallop, wallop! There's gnomes heads all over the lawn, but by the time anyone notices, the jogger has gone! Right. What time are they arrivin'? When Roger an' Jane get here we'll have to be on the lookout for clues, little things like a lump hammer in her handbag or...

PAULINE Why do you always laugh at Jane?

DENNIS Who's laughin'?

PAULINE You are, Dennis, and I'm getting fed up with it. When we moved up here to Phase Two Jane could easily have ignored us, pretended that she didn't know us. But she didn't. She made sure that we were included. Jane made sure that we were accepted on this estate.

DENNIS (assuming a mock American film-trailer voice) Jane, a woman... or a legend? Jane, the fabulous female of Phase Two. Before I met Jane I was just a quivering working-class slob. Before I met Jane I thought lasagne was a swedish actress, before I met Jane... No! There was no "before"...

The telephone rings. DENNIS *answers it.*

(on the phone) Hell... (To PAULINE) Phone box... Five-oh-oh-nine... Hiya ma!

PAULINE Is that your mother? Here... (She takes the phone from him)

DENNIS *goes into the kitchen.*

(on the phone) Mother...you were supposed to be getting here early... But I told you to get off at the first bus stop. (Covering the receiver and shouting to DENNIS) Dennis, they've got lost, they've got off at the wrong bus stop again. (On the phone) Mother, you've been to the bungalow God knows how many times, why can't you or Dad remember where it is? ...Oh no, they do not all look alike... We do not have a number, Mother, because we do not like to deface the façade of the bungalow... Look, exactly where are you? ...Right, now go out of Brahms Close and take the first right into Sibelius Street. At Elgar Drive, turn right, go past Mahler Crescent, till you get to the Beethoven Underpass. When you come up from the Underpass you'll see Wagner Walkway right in front of you... That's right...yes... and Symphony Avenue is just on the left...that's right we're three houses down from Torville Dene... No, no number! ...just "The Haven" ...that's right, "The Haven" ...We'll see you... Oh Mother, mother... Do you think Dad will like hachis au parmentier?

DENNIS *comes in from the kitchen carrying a can of lager.*

She's just asking him... Hello... Hello? ... *(She replaces the receiver)*

DENNIS Well? Does he like hachis au parmentier?

PAULINE He asked if that was the pebble-dashed semi on the corner.

DENNIS Well why didn't you tell her it was cottage pie?

PAULINE Because Dennis, it is not cottage pie, it is "hachis au parmentier". Oh, Dennis, you're not drinking already are you? I don't want you getting drunk. You get loud when you're drunk. Why don't you drink in moderation, like Roger?

DENNIS Have you seen the amount Roger gets through? Roger drinks like Margaret Thatcher promises tax cuts—often, indiscriminately and always at the expense of others.

PAULINE But he doesn't become loud with it. At least Roger approaches alcohol as an aid to social interaction and not as an aid to lunacy.

DENNIS But I like lunacy.

PAULINE All right, but come on, there's lots to do before they arrive. It is for your birthday that we're having this dinner, the least you could do is help get things ready.

DENNIS What d' y' want doin'?

PAULINE Have you cleared up that mess in the hall yet?

DENNIS Which mess?

PAULINE There's your old haversack lying all over the place.

DENNIS Rucksack.

PAULINE You could put that away for a start. *(She goes into the kitchen)* We're not taking it to Spain with us if that's what you think. You can't get on a shiny new jet with an old rucksack. I don't know why you took it out in the first place.

DENNIS I took it out because I wanted to look at it and feel it and put me head inside it and smell its smells of diesel oil and grass and Anglesey and beer and Edinburgh and old perfumes and sea salt and sand.

Pause.

Who put moth balls in it?

PAULINE *enters from the kitchen. She is looking for something.*

PAULINE ...Table mats... *(Thinking)* Oh, I know... *(She goes to the bureau and tries to open it only to find that it is locked)* Dennis... I can't get into the bureau. Dennis, I need the table mats. Dennis, it's locked.

DENNIS I know.

PAULINE Well where's the key?

DENNIS You want table mats? *(He goes to the bureau and opens it whilst concealing its contents)*

PAULINE Dennis, what's in there? Why do you keep it locked? What's in...

DENNIS *(handing her the table mats)* Nothing.

PAULINE Well, why keep it locked if...

DENNIS Me poems. I keep me poems in there. I do still write, you know.

PAULINE But why do you keep them locked away?

DENNIS I keep me poems locked away, Pauline, *(conspiratorially)* in case someone tries to steal them.

PAULINE *(laughing, relieved)* Oh Dennis... *(She embraces him)* Who'd want to steal your poetry?

DENNIS Pauline... Who'd want to graft arms on to a Venus de Milo?

PAULINE Do you really still write poems?

DENNIS *nods.*

Sometimes I take out your old poems and read them. They make me sad.

DENNIS Why?

PAULINE I don't know. Things were just...just easier then weren't they? I mean, I know we didn't have the same...things then, a car, a beautiful home...

DENNIS ...a marvellous microwave, digital dishwasher, vacuum cleaner, dimmer switches...hachis au parmentier... I'll tell you what I'll do—for your next birthday, I'll write you a new poem. Would you like that?

PAULINE *(nodding, smiling)* Ah, Dennis. That'll be lovely, thank you.

DENNIS Don't thank me...saved me a hundred and twenty quid. I *was* gonna get you a new sewing machine.

The phone rings. **DENNIS** *answers it.*

PAULINE Oh no...

DENNIS Hello, five-oh-oh- ...Hello Dad, that chest's not so good is it? Go on, take it easy, get y' breath back first... That's better, go on... So, exactly where are you now? ...Erm no, no that's not exactly nearer...erm, it sounds to me as though you've wandered into the adjoining estate... Yeh...yeh I know they all look alike... Listen, have you found that little pub on the corner? That's right, *The Crotchet and Quaver*... Well, go up the pedestrian precinct *(spelling it out)* Pedestrian precinct... The street, go up the street... Listen it'd be much easier if y' just let me pick y' up in the car...yes, I know me mother gets indigestion if she has to travel in a car. Well look...just, just get back onto the other side of the road and follow the instructions Pauline gave you... All right, OK we might see y' by next Christmas then? Tarrah.

PAULINE Dennis, what are we going to do? I wanted to have them here early so that we could get them settled in before Jane and Roger arrive. What are we going to do?

DENNIS Just pray that they turn back before they reach the Pennines.

PAULINE exits to the kitchen and DENNIS puts on a record at low volume.

PAULINE You know how Jane always casts a critical eye on things. Dennis have you opened the wine yet?

DENNIS What for? There's no one here yet.

PAULINE comes back from the kitchen.

PAULINE Dennis, what is wrong with you? Surely you've learnt by now that wine needs time to breathe.

DENNIS Breathe? It's Italian plonk on special offer. That lot wouldn't breathe if it was in an oxygen tent.

PAULINE What's wrong with you? You've been in this mood all day haven't you?

He stares at her.

Ah, I'm sorry if I'm moaning at you, Dennis, but you won't take anything seriously. Tomorrow Den, you'll be thirty-five—you're a father and a mortgagee. I mean, I used to laugh at your antics as much as anyone when we were young. But we're not young any longer, Den, but you're still acting as if you were, and Dennis, it's really not fitting.

She looks at him and realizes that he hasn't been listening to a word.

Dennis, are you listening to me?

He merely stares, absorbed.

Dennis, I'm taking time off from the kitchen to talk to you an' you're not even listening to...

DENNIS Listen.

PAULINE What?

DENNIS Listen... Listen to that.

PAULINE Listen to what Dennis?

He goes to the stereo and replaces the needle on the track. He turns up the volume and we listen to the verse before he turns the volume down again.

DENNIS *(reciting the verse we have just heard)* Richard got married to a figure skater/An' he bought her a dishwasher and a coffee percolator/And he drinks at home now/most nights with the TV on/And all the house lights turned up bright.

PAULINE Well?

DENNIS That's me.

PAULINE Who?

DENNIS Us. You're the figure skater and I'm Richard.

PAULINE But you're Dennis.

DENNIS And Richard. Richard. That *is* me, isn't it?

PAULINE Dennis, I don't know what you're going on about. *(Returning to the kitchen)* But if you're going to change your name it's not going to be Richard. I'm not having people rushing round this bungalow shouting out "Dick".

DENNIS *(more to himself than* **PAULINE***)* The song...it's about a feller who used to drink in the bars. And the girl loved him but...for some reason they went their separate ways until years later when they run into each other again. And the feller, Richard, who used to drink in the bars and sing with his crowd and talk and talk and talk, about what him and the rest of them were going to do, where they were going to go, well...he hasn't done any of it. He hasn't gone anywhere. When the girl knew him, they'd all been young and where they were all headed to was somewhere good and alive and continuing. But when the girl meets him again... He doesn't drink in the bars now. He just goes down to the corner and gets a six pack and takes it back home. He drinks it with the telly flickering before him and all the house lights turned up bright.

PAULINE *(from the kitchen)* What happens to the girl?

DENNIS It...it doesn't say. It's not about the girl. It's about him, the song, not her.

PAULINE Ah yeh, but it's all right for him, isn't it?

DENNIS Why?

PAULINE Well, I mean, he's settled down hasn't he? He's got a house and everything. But what's the girl ended up with? Is she married?

DENNIS I don't know.

PAULINE Yeh. See what I mean. Hey Den, why don't you play your guitar these days? Mm? I used to like it when you gave us a song. Why don't you play it anymore?

DENNIS Hey, maybe I will. I could get it out the garage tonight, put some new string on it...

PAULINE Agh, not tonight, Dennis. Not when we've got people coming. Put a record on if you want some music. Let's have something classical—let's have Richard Clayderman. No, perhaps not. Classical might be a bit heavy for a Saturday. Oh Dennis, put John Denver on. Nobody could take exception to John Denver.

DENNIS I could. I hate John Denver.

PAULINE Dennis, you love John Denver.

DENNIS I do not. I have got a glorious loathing of John Denver.

PAULINE Well you used to like him. You used to try and comb your hair to look like John Denver's.

DENNIS Pauline, I'd rather have any hair in the world other than John Denver's—even Arthur Scargill's.

PAULINE But you used to be so fond of John Denver.

DENNIS Well, now I hate him.

PAULINE Dennis, don't keep saying "hate". If you don't like him you could at least say "detest".

DENNIS But I don't "detest" him.

PAULINE I told you.

DENNIS I "hate" him. Hate, hate, hate, hate, hate.

PAULINE You carry on like that and you'll have Val next door hearing you. She's very fond of him.

DENNIS *goes to the window, opens it and shouts out.*

DENNIS I, Dennis Cain, of The Haven wish it to be known that I have a passionate and terrible hatred of John, Goldilocks, Denver.

PAULINE *enters from the kitchen and begins to struggle with him to get him away from the window.*

John Denver should be garrotted with his own G string and...

PAULINE *finally manages to pull him away.*

PAULINE Dennis. Have you gone mad? What are you trying to do? Shouting stuff like that... My God, don't you realize how many people you could upset? John Denver's very well thought of on this estate. *(As she closes the window)* Oh no...there's Val. Hello Val. Yes I thought I heard someone shouting too. That's why we were looking out. I think it came from your side, Val...

DENNIS Definitely your side, Val.

PAULINE Ah yeh, that's true, it probably was them. You know what they're like, those Parnes kids.

DENNIS They want throttlin', Val.

PAULINE I'll have some strong words for them when I see them again... OK, Val. Bye.

DENNIS Bye, Val. Y' know, you could get to feel very sorry for those poor bloody Parnes kids.

PAULINE Well, what do you expect me to do? Tell her the truth? Oh, don't worry Val, it was just Dennis treating the estate to his opinion of John Denver. Well I hope for your sake that Roger and Jane didn't hear you. John Denver's a god in *their* eyes.

The telephone rings.

Dennis, you get it. Look at the time and I'm not even changed yet.

PAULINE *exits.*

DENNIS *(on the phone)* Hello, Control Tower... No, it's me Mother... Dennis. Control Tower? It was a joke. Well... I know it's nothing to laugh at... Well, if you'd let me pick you up in the car... I know you get indigestion in cars... yes I know everywhere looks the same on these estates... Mother, you're lucky, a woman went out for a loaf of bread once an' was gone for six months. Look, did you find *The Crotchet and Quaver?* That's where you're phoning from? Right, look... Get someone to direct you to the hypermarket and you'll see a phone there. Telephone when you get there an' I'll fetch the car for you... No, Mother, you won't have to travel in the car if you don't want to... I'll drive very slowly and you an' me Dad can follow the tail lights...

The door chimes play a snatch of the William Tell Overture.

I'll have to go Mother, the Lone Ranger's at the door. Tarrah. Good luck.

DENNIS *exits to the front door.*

(offstage) Aye, aye.

ROGER All right, kid.

JANE Evening, Dennis.

> **DENNIS** *enters followed by* **JANE** *and* **ROGER**. **ROGER** *is carrying a bottle of wine and a birthday present.*

DENNIS Pauline's just gettin' changed.

JANE Not ready when her guests arrive? A little black mark for Pauline.

ROGER Black mark for herself, eh?

JANE It's a good thing you're entertaining us and not some of the others I could think of on this estate. You know that some people would hold a mistake like that against you for life.

DENNIS Jane, that very thought crossed my mind as I opened the door. How lucky we are, I said to myself, how lucky we are that it's only Jane and Roger!

ROGER *(handing* **DENNIS** *the wine)* There y' go, kid. Brought y'a little bottle of somethin'.

DENNIS Ta, Rodge. Red. I'll put it by the cooker to keep warm.

JANE Warm? Dennis, that is Beaujolais Nouveau. I thought everybody knew that Beaujolais is the one red wine which must be served chilled.

DENNIS Oh, of course, trust me. Chilled it must be. Well, Jane, I'm sure, if you held on to it for half an hour...!

ROGER It's the only red wine we drink in summer, isn't it love? You know what they say about red wine in summer don't you kid? "In summer, big bold burgundies should be abandoned".

DENNIS I shun them, Rodge!

ROGER *(producing the box-like, wrapped object)* Now kid, bought y'a little pressy. Here. You'll love it. He'll love it won't he?

DENNIS Thanks, Rodge. Ta, Jane. *(He begins to unwrap it)*

JANE Mum and Dad not here yet, Dennis? I was just saying to Roger, it must be years since I saw them.

DENNIS It might be years still. *(He unwraps the gift to reveal a record-carrying case)* Ogh, thanks. A record-carrying case.

JANE Look inside, Dennis.

DENNIS *(lifting the lid)* Oh. *(Without enthusiasm)* A record as well.

ROGER You'll never guess who it's by, kid.

DENNIS I think I might just, Rodge.

JANE Well, there's no need to guess, Dennis—just take it out and have a look.

DENNIS Do I have to?

JANE Not if you don't want to see your present.

ROGER He's just savourin' the moment, aren't y', kid?

DENNIS Yeh.

ROGER Well...go on, go on.

DENNIS *(pulling out the record)* John Denver.

ROGER 'Ey, double album that is. Take y' two hours to get through that.

DENNIS Fabulous.

    PAULINE *enters.*

PAULINE Hello, everyone.

ROGER Ogh... Now look at that. You look great, kidder. Doesn't she look magic?

JANE That's a lovely little dress, Pauline.

PAULINE Thank you, Jane. Oh, Dennis, what's that?

DENNIS It's a present, from Jane and Roger.

PAULINE Ogh...a record-carrying case. Isn't that lovely. When you go out you'll be able to take all your records with you.

DENNIS Take them for a walk.

PAULINE Ogh, and a record as well. What is it? *(She takes out the record, sees what it is, drops it back and slams the case shut)* No one's got a drink. Who'd like a drink? Dennis what are you doing not offering our guests a drink?

JANE *(laughing)* Another black mark, Dennis.

DENNIS Another one. If we carry on like this it'll be the firing squad for us won't it? Lined up at dawn, in Sainsbury's car park an' shot by a platoon of the best hostesses on the estate.

PAULINE Dennis, will you please offer Jane and Roger a drink?

DENNIS Ah...but, my love, it seems that when I purchased the said red I was forgetting that in summer big bold burgundies should be abandoned. Trust me to forget that. That's obviously why it was on special offer. Everyone else on the estate knows of the summer burgundy curse, but not me. I rush in and buy up seventeen litres of the stuff. Well, at least there'll be something to look forward to when winter comes. That's if we last that long, now that we've got seventy-nine black marks in the book and an evening of desperate sobriety ahead, Jane what do you prefer, cock or penis?

PAULINE Dennis!

JANE Oh, don't worry Pauline. I'm used to him. Anyway, he can't fool me—I know there are no such wines on the market.

ROGER Anyway, kid, we don't mind drinkin' red. I mean, we're not exactly connoisseurs. What we said about the burgundies, we just read it in the paper last Sunday.

JANE I didn't read it in the paper.

ROGER We did, love.

JANE *(an Exocet glance)* Roger, you may well have done. But I did not. For as long as I can remember, I have known about the big bold burgundies.

ROGER But I remember...

JANE Roger.

DENNIS Watch it, Roger.

JANE Anyway don't you think there are more important matters than wine to discuss?

ROGER Oh aye. I'd forgotten.

PAULINE What is it? Jane what's wrong?

JANE My God, is nothing sacred? Are we all to be brought down by the times in which we live? Are we all to be victims of this sickness?

PAULINE Jane...?

JANE It's wicked. It's mindless.

PAULINE What's happened?

DENNIS What's up then, flower?

ROGER Don't push her, kid. She's had a shock, we both have.

JANE I don't really know if I can bear to talk about it.

DENNIS Well if you don't tell us how are we to discuss it, Jane?

ROGER I think kid, with what's been goin' on lately, you just might be able to guess.

DENNIS Oh no, Rodge, not that!

PAULINE What, Dennis, what?

DENNIS Is that it, Jane? I've guessed it. Oh, what a black day. So. Barry Manilow's going to have a nose job. A government spokesman has said that this could solve Britain's unemployment problems.

PAULINE Dennis shut up!

ROGER Don't shout at him, kidder. It's not his fault.

JANE You mock Dennis, but you might be next.

DENNIS Next what?

ROGER The next victim, kid, the next victim.

Pause.

Y' know what we woke up to this mornin'? Broke my heart, didn't it love? Shocked I was.

JANE The entire garden...defiled.

DENNIS Get away.

PAULINE How?

ROGER Y' know that row of cabbages, Dennis, them with the lovely little hearts in them? Everyone of them covered in paint.

PAULINE No.

JANE But not painted at random Pauline, oh no.

ROGER No. Not content with mere vandalism this lot had to display their artistic talents as well... Those grand little cabbage hearts had been painted to look like...well...like, well I'll be frank...like breasts.

PAULINE Well, what a thing to do.

ROGER For the sake of decency I'll not tell y' what they did to my organic cucumbers.

DENNIS Roger, Roger, what's decency at a time like this...did they paint your cucumbers to look like...

JANE There hadn't been an ounce of chemicals on those vegetables, had there, Roger?

ROGER Pure, my soil is. Pure. You could eat off that soil. Surgeons could operate in my garden. It's true.

PAULINE And have you lost all your little organic vegetables?

ROGER Oh no, they'll still grow, Pauline love. But that's not the point is it? I mean what are we gonna do when we have people round to dinner? You know our dining table faces the garden. Many a guest has lingered over coffee and been moved to comment upon the state of my garden. But what we gonna do now? Ey? We can hardly have our bloody guests sittin' there starin' out at a row of tits an' pricks can we?

JANE Roger. Language!

ROGER Well...we're all adults. Anyway, it makes you swear.

JANE I suppose that now we'll just have to eat with the blinds drawn.

DENNIS Couldn't y' just move the table?

ROGER Who? Not me Dennis. That's what they want us to do Dennis. Intimidation. That's what they'd like. They'd like to see us move our dining room table but if we do that we've lost out to them. No, I will not move the table. I will sit, where I've always sat. I don't seek martyrdom but if it's thrust upon me in this manner then I must respond. It's my duty to respond.

PAULINE Jane, who do you think is responsible?

JANE I would have thought that was obvious Pauline. It's those Parnes kids, isn't it?

DENNIS Jane, the Parnes kids are aged three, four, seven and nine.

PAULINE But they're very big for their age, Dennis.

DENNIS What?

JANE And Mr Parnes, you know what he is don't you?

DENNIS Go on.

JANE Tell him Roger.

ROGER An art teacher!

JANE And you've seen her, have you, Pauline?

PAULINE Mrs?

JANE Yes.

DENNIS What's wrong with her?

JANE Dennis, Dennis. Wellingtons in summer? CND badge?

DENNIS So. Years ago you used to wear a CND badge.

JANE When we did it, Dennis, we did it because it was fun!
It's not the same today.

DENNIS But that doesn't mean...

JANE I think it does, Dennis...

ROGER Anarchists, all of them. A paint brush in one hand, an
aerosol can in the other.

PAULINE A what?

DENNIS Anyone like a drink?

ROGER An aerosol spray, love. The trademark of the vandal,
of the anarchist.

DENNIS Big bold burgundies all round eh? I know it's summer
an' all that but if we use our imagination we might just be
able to pour a gallon or two down our throats.

DENNIS *takes some glasses and exits to the kitchen.*

ROGER One of the worst things you know, is that I have to
admit they did a good job. Sore and bitter though I was,
the artist in me couldn't fail to see that it was well done.
Them cabbage hearts have got recognizable nipples on them.

JANE That's the most distressing thing about this whole wave of
vandalism—there's something ominously creative about it.

DENNIS *enters with drinks.*

DENNIS Here we go...

ROGER They'll not get my greenhouse though.

DENNIS Have you taken it down, Rodge?

ROGER I have not taken it down and I will not be taking it down. But whoever wants to get at my greenhouse now will have to get past a six foot fence with barbed wire on top.

JANE And after tomorrow they'll have the force to cope with.

PAULINE The police force?

JANE The police force? What good is the police force? Have you seen the police force lately, Pauline? It's full of little men, with beards. No, I mean the residents' force, Pauline. I've told Roger it's the only way. He's organized a meeting for tomorrow. Haven't you, Roger?

ROGER Well, as I said love, there's no point rushing headlong into...

JANE The meeting is at our house.

ROGER 'Cos there's all sorts of problems that have to be looked...

JANE At two o'clock.

ROGER Two o'clock the meetin' is. You will be there won't y' Den?

JANE Of course Dennis will be there. We all know that in the past Dennis has avoided joining any of the clubs or committees, but that was at a time of peace. In war it's different. Isn't it Dennis? At a time of crisis we band together, don't we? We unite in order to protect what is ours. Don't we?

DENNIS *remains dumb.*

Unless, that is, we happen to be some sort of a freak!

ROGER CADAVARS the organization is to be called— "Castlehills Against Destruction Anarchy Vandalism And Riot Society" —I thought of that. I reckon it could be a good thing for Phase Two residents to get involved in somethin' like this. There's lots of chaps who I met who are bored to death an' somethin' like this could be a godsend. I reckon it could catch on in a big way. The possibilities are endless once we've got goin'. If we really got organized we could offer all sorts of facilities—diving and swimming instruction, driving...

DENNIS Commando training in the park, SAS classes, air/sea rescue, ski-ing, helicopter piloting, aerobics, brain surgery...

ROGER We could even have a junior section, get the kids involved.

JANE Roger, we're forming a protection force—not a youth club.

ROGER Yeh, but I think this could be a good idea, getting the kids involved, especially the likes of the Parnes kids. We might as well put their artistic talents to some use. We'll need someone to design an' print leaflets, draw up posters...

JANE Roger, what point is there in having a movement like CADAVARS if we bring all the vandals into it? Mm?

ROGER I never thought of it like that.

JANE No, no, some vandals must be kept on the outside.

PAULINE Dennis, where have your parents got to?

DENNIS Bombay? Karakas? No, they've probably been arrested by one of Roger's special task force. I'll bet me Mum an' Dad are bein' interrogated right now. Vat ees zee purpose of zees meesteerious phone calls? Vat ees meant by "Ze Haven"? Who ees zee krut you call parmentier?

PAULINE If they're not here soon the hachis au parmentier is going to be...

JANE Oh, have you tried hachis, love? That is a brave step... But a step in the right direction. A woman who serves hachis au parmentier is a woman on the right path. Let's have a little look shall we?

PAULINE *and* **JANE** *exit to the kitchen.*

ROGER Hachis what?

DENNIS Cottage pie, don't worry. *(He goes to the stereo)* Come here. Listen to this.

ROGER What is it? Somethin' new?

DENNIS Not really. Listen. *(He plays the verse from "THE LAST TIME I SAW RICHARD")*

ROGER Not bad, not bad.

DENNIS Did you hear it though? Did you hear what she said?

ROGER What was that he bought for her?

DENNIS A dishwasher and a coffee pecolator. Rodge, that's me.

ROGER Now let me get this right, you've bought Pauline a dishwasher.

DENNIS No, the feller, in the song. It's me.

ROGER Is that right, Dennis?

DENNIS Do you know what I did today?

ROGER If your Saturday was anything like mine you spent most of it pushing a wire trolley around a hypermarket tellin' yourself that any moment some tantalizing and uninhibited feminist will accost you and recognize immediately your dedication to sexual equality by virtue of the fact that you obviously know your way around the store and thus must always do the shopping. Turned on to unknown heights by this discovery of a truly non-sexist male she will insist on having you there and then amidst the bin bags and the frozen pizzas.

DENNIS No.

ROGER No, it didn't happen to me either. But you've got to think of somethin' when you're out shoppin'.

DENNIS Rodge, what happened was... I was out in the car. I had to go past the motorway slip road. Have you ever seen them down there? People, fellers and women, with rucksacks and sleepin' rolls, lining up at the side of the road, hitching, goin' away. I turned the car round and drove back to the slip road. I pulled in and parked and I sat for ages just watchin' them gettin' lifts, goin', one by one, away to anywhere. I wanted to get out of the car, leave it behind and take me place in the queue of hitch-hikers.

ROGER What the bloody hell do you want to do somethin' like that for?

DENNIS Rodge, I'll be thirty-five tomorrow; halfway through the game Rodge, the first half all played and only the second half left. *(Pause)* Don't you remember what it was like, years ago, listenin' to Dylan all through the night? Don't you remember that? Don't y??

ROGER Course I do.

DENNIS Remember what we were all gonna do, all the plans we made? How we were gonna spend our lives?

ROGER He's gone all religious, Dylan.

DENNIS But don't you remember? Don't you think back to the promises we made?

ROGER I was gonna be a famous singer wasn't I? Was gonna light up the world, me. But there's no point dwellin' on all that is there? I've got a good life here. What's the point in allowin' yourself to become dissatisfied?

DENNIS You had a great voice, Rodge. I thought you'd made it you know. You disappeared for years an' I thought you were out there somewhere, making it big. When I moved to Phase Two, I didn't expect to find you here Rodge.

ROGER You got it wrong, Dennis. I could sing a song all right but I was only average.

DENNIS No, everyone said Rodge. You were good. You could have made it.

ROGER No.

DENNIS You could.

ROGER I know. But...but. I'm always tellin' the kids y' know I'm always tellin' Michael an Amanda. "You think," I say to them, "you think I just bloody sell double glazin' an' mow the lawn. But your father," I say... "Your father could have been a great singer, a famous man." Mind you, Dennis, I say "could" but who knows, one day I may still do it.

DENNIS You won't, Rodge. None of us will.

ROGER How do you know?

DENNIS You won't, Rodge. It's too late. You've given up.

ROGER Says who?

DENNIS Says me.

ROGER Well you're wrong kid, you're bloody wrong.

DENNIS Am I, Rodge?

ROGER *(rattled)* Listen, if I've given up why the soddin hell do I always play a famous singer when we're playin' Wogan?

DENNIS When you're doin' what?

ROGER Play Wogan. Y' know what I mean.

DENNIS I don't.

ROGER Come off it, Dennis. You mean you never play the Wogan game?

DENNIS No.

ROGER See...think you know everythin' but when it comes down to it, you're right out of bloody touch aren't y', Dennis. They all do it round here. It's the new thing.

DENNIS Well, what is it you do for Christ's sake?

ROGER You play out the interview don't y'? Like, when me an' Jane do it, she plays the part of Wogan, an' I play the part of me, when I'm famous. Some of them round here play Russell Harty but I don't think it's as good. Look, come on, I'll show y'. *(He begins to move around the furniture*

in order to create a studio interview set) Y' don't know a
bloody thing that goes on, do y'? In social matters, Dennis,
you're a nomark. But old Rodge'll show y' what it's about.
Right, now that's Terry's chair there. Now you sit there an'
be Terry. I know you won't be able to do a perfect impression
of him at this stage, you're just a beginner. Jane's Wogan is
bloody wonderful you know. A spectacle to behold. Right,
come on Terry, come on Wogie, come on...

DENNIS *sits down, bewildered.*

Now, I'll come on as me, when I'm famous. Right, let's get
this show on the road. *(He moves to the side of the room so
as to make an entrance into the "studio" and improvizes the
Wogan theme, as he does so)* Come on, kid... Wogan, Wogan...

DENNIS What do I do?

ROGER Be him, be him. Right... Now introduce me.

DENNIS You and Jane do this?

ROGER I've told y'. Everyone does it.

DENNIS In your front room?

ROGER Of course. Now come on, be him. *(He again improvizes
the Wogan theme)* Camera one over there. *(Pointing)* You're
out of shot kid, Camera one, camera one, over there kid...
that's right...

DENNIS *faces front and adjusts himself to face the studio
audience.*

DENNIS Hello and welcome. On my show tonight a man who has
risen from the very depths of nowhere to find himself where
he is today; that is the very pinnacle of the entertainment
industry.

ROGER That's it, kid...great, great.

DENNIS He's a fellow who has won not only the love of the
public, but also the respect of his colleagues in the world

of show business. An international star, a world celebrity...
in short, a superstar.

ROGER Ogh, wonderful kid. You're a natural.

DENNIS A rare phenomenon. A creature unique in the annals
of show business.

ROGER *preens himself.*

But my first guest tonight...

ROGER *is stung.*

...is Roger Fuller.

ROGER Now look here, Dennis...

DENNIS Come on, you're on, you're on...

ROGER *makes his entrance, providing his own signature
tune and applause.*

Welcome...welcome. Roger, I believe congratulations are
due to you in respect of your latest sell-out concert at New
York's Madison Square Garden, where I hear you were joined
on stage by John Denver.

ROGER That's right, Terry. John just called me up the day of
the concert an' we were chewin' a little fat y' know an' ...

DENNIS 'Scuse me, excuse me. You were chewing a little fat
what?

ROGER Y' what?

DENNIS It was a joke. "A little fat what?"

ROGER Look kid, I do the jokes. When Jane plays Wogan she
plays Wogan without the jokes. I get the jokes.

DENNIS Now Roger, you were tellin' us about Madison Sq...

ROGER Well, it's like I was tellin' y' Terry, John called me up an'
he knew about my concert an' he said it would be a great
privilege for him if he could join me onstage an' I thought

that was kinda neat y' know. Ah he's a big fan of mine. You know he's doin' an album of my songs in the fall?

DENNIS No, I didn't know that, Roger. I'll have to look out for it.

ROGER Yeh, John and me we been...

DENNIS Yes, we'll come back to that a little later. Erm. For the moment I'd like to put to you a question that I know most of my viewers would like an answer to, and it's this, Roger. In your line of business, do you get a lot of women to screw?

ROGER Ey, hold on, hold on. Wogan wouldn't ask a question like that.

DENNIS He'd want to, though.

ROGER He might want to. But he wouldn't bloody do it on the air.

DENNIS *(to "audience")* Do you know I don't think he's goin' to answer the question.

ROGER I can't answer that. Ask proper Wogan questions.

DENNIS OK. OK. Let's go back to that concert.

ROGER That's more like it. That's it kid. Go on.

DENNIS Now a little birdie told me that when Denver came on stage he was greeted with most of the audience walking out in protest.

ROGER That's not true.

DENNIS And this little birdie went on to say that when you started to sing together the remainder of the audience walked out as well.

ROGER Hold on, hold on.

DENNIS And that Denver and yourself ended up singing to the usherettes, all of whom were fast asleep by the end of the show.

ROGER I don't have to put up with this. I'm leaving.

DENNIS I'm sorry to insist on this but...

ROGER Y' know what you are on't y? Y' just a bog Irish bollock who knows sod all about nowt. Russell Harty could knock you sideways.

DENNIS Agh, come on Rodge, I was just gettin' into it then.

ROGER No, I've had enough. You're no good. You'll never get the hang of it, kid. You're got to understand the personality of the man before you can do it justice.

DENNIS Ah, Rodge, come on, it's good this...

JANE enters with more drinks.

JANE What's all the noise for?

DENNIS It's him.

ROGER It's him. I'm tryin' to teach him how to play the Wogan game but he's useless. He'll never get it.

JANE The Wogan Game?

ROGER Wogan, the game we play.

JANE Oh. That silly game you sometimes play with the children.

PAULINE enters.

PAULINE Dennis, where are your parents? If they're not here soon the dinner's going to be ruined.

DENNIS Just leave it in the oven.

JANE Dennis, there are some dishes which will survive a spell in the oven but I'm afraid hachis au parmentier is not one of them.

DENNIS But if they haven't arrived, they haven't arrived.

PAULINE But it's not fair, Dennis, they're always doing this.

DENNIS All right, all right... I'll get the car out and see if I can find them.

ROGER Want me to come with y', kid? Case y' meet any hitch-hikers?

DENNIS No. You stay near the phone, Rodge. If Wogan rings, tell him I'm not available.

DENNIS *exits.*

ROGER Mind if I help meself to another big bold burgundy, kidder?

PAULINE I'll get it for...

ROGER No, y' won't pet. You sit there. I'm a liberated man, I am, y' know. You'll not see me sittin' around expectin' women to wait upon me hand and foot, will you Jane?

JANE Roger, just go and get your drink please.

ROGER I have beaten the two big Cs of our time Pauline, chauvinism...and cholestrol. *(He makes his exit to the kitchen)*

PAULINE I do like Roger. *(Pause)* I mean, as a friend.

JANE Doesn't everybody Pauline. He's a very popular man.

Unseen by **JANE** *and* **PAULINE.** **DENNIS** *enters and unlocks the bureau. He takes out aerosol cans and exits.*

PAULINE He's always in demand, isn't he?

JANE Always, Pauline. I think it's his great warmth that so many people respond to. And his strength, this...inner strength which seems, somehow, to communicate itself to those around him.

PAULINE And you're very happy together, aren't you?

JANE Intensely, Pauline. And you know the main reason for that, don't you? I know it's basic, but it's true—Roger and I have a wonderful sex life. Wonderful.

PAULINE Oh. Erm...good.

JANE And do you know why that is? Because in our love-making we leave nothing to chance. *(She beams at* **PAULINE***)* Sex, Pauline, sex can be a wonderful thing—if it's organized.

PAULINE Well...yes... I suppose...

JANE Now, don't get me wrong. Roger is a ram. Yes.

PAULINE Oh.

JANE Very demanding Pauline. Very. He's lusty. A big, lusty man.

ROGER *enters, bearing a glass brimming with red wine.*

ROGER 'Ey, it's good stuff this, kidder. Y' get the taste after a few.

JANE Roger!

ROGER What?

JANE *indicates to* ROGER *that he should get out but he fails to realize.*

JANE Roger! How many times have I told you that when drinking wine you have to leave room in the glass for the bouquet?

ROGER Ah. *(He swallows the drink in one)* Done. *(He sniffs the glass)* There. A lovely bouquet.

JANE Roger, go and see how the dinner's getting on.

ROGER Eh?

JANE Roger. Get out.

ROGER Oh... Oh... *(He exits to the kitchen)*

PAULINE A big lusty man, Pauline. But what good is untutored lust? Mm? No good. It has to be harnessed, orchestrated until one achieves a real symphony of sex. Don't be shocked, Pauline.

PAULINE I'm not, Jane.

JANE Because if you are going to solve your problems one of the first things you're going to have to do is learn how to talk freely about those problems.

PAULINE Jane, which problems?

JANE You poor love. God, what you must be suffering.

PAULINE Jane, what do you...

JANE Reading is also highly important. Not pornography—that I would not recommend. I mean material written by people with expert medical knowledge, authentic sexologists. *The Joy of Sex* by Dr Alex B. Comfort—*A Gourmet Guide To Love-Making.* The problems that you and Dennis are facing alone can be beaten with a friend at hand. Premature, is he? Premature? Far more common that you'd think Pauline.

PAULINE No, I'm sure Dennis was carried for the full nine months.

JANE As common as the common cold but the cause of far greater misery. But it can be cured Pauline, simply. In some cases it's merely a question of underpants.

PAULINE Pardon?

JANE Yes. Underpants! I'll bet he wears them extremely tight, doesn't he Pauline, doesn't he? Tight, around the crotch, jockey style, displaying his outlines. Am I right, Pauline? Of course I'm right. You see, it's un-natural for them to be so hemmed in, Pauline. Get him into boxer shorts, Pauline, and your terrible problem will be solved.

PAULINE But... Jane, we haven't got a sexual problem.

JANE *(laughing)* Oh, Pauline, the marriages that have floundered with the partners echoing those very words.

PAULINE But Jane, we haven't.

JANE *(beaming sympathy)* Haven't you?

PAULINE *(a little worried)* I don't think so.

JANE You mean to tell me that there's been nothing strange about Dennis's behaviour. Nothing a little, out of the ordinary?

PAULINE Well he, he...but it can't be anything to do with sex.

JANE You let me be the judge of that. Now I want you to tell me everything.

PAULINE Well it's just... it's just that he keeps something, in the bureau and he says it's his poetry...but I know it's not. It's something else.

JANE What?

PAULINE Jane, I don't know.

JANE Then why don't you look?

PAULINE He keeps it locked. He won't let me have the key.

JANE *(staring at the offending bureau)* But this is preposterous.

PAULINE I know.

JANE *(moving towards the suspicious item of furniture and eyeing it)* This cannot be allowed to continue. *(Pointing)* In there. You mean there's something in there?

PAULINE Yes.

JANE Right. Let's have it open.

PAULINE But Jane, Dennis keeps the key in...

JANE Do you have a crowbar?

PAULINE Oh, Jane, I couldn't...

JANE Pauline, this is not allowed. In a marriage the only secrets are murky secrets. Fetch a crowbar.

PAULINE Jane, Jane I can't...

JANE But I can. Fetch me a crowbar.

PAULINE But if the lock's forced Dennis will know and...

JANE *(raising her hands)* All right, Pauline, all right. If you want to leave it then fine, fine. If you want to live in mystery then that's up to you, but I'm telling you now—when men start locking cupboards and drawers then, mark my words, there's only one thing they can be hiding.

PAULINE *(alarmed)* What?

JANE Pornography. Stand back. *(She goes into an expert Kung Fu stance)*

PAULINE *rushes forward to shield the bureau.*

Pauline, don't you understand what it is you're protecting?

PAULINE Yes, a genuine Queen Anne Bureau.

JANE Reproduction, Pauline, reproduction.

PAULINE All right, genuine reproduction, but we can't just smash it open.

JANE Pauline, I give you my word there will be no splinters. One blow, that's all it needs, one blow, delivered with precision. The insides of that bureau are seething with filth, bulging with the unspeakable. Pauline, what's he been filling his mind with? And if he's not stopped now, what's to be next? I'll tell you what's next, flashing his privates in the shopping arcade, breathing heavily down telephone lines, wearing knickers, silk knickers purchased from Janet Reger and delivered under cover of plain paper. Underpants! He wears knickers, doesn't he, Pauline, silk knickers?

PAULINE No, NO!

JANE Then he's got nothing to hide. Stand back.

PAULINE *moves to one side as* JANE *summons up all her power and lunges. She Kung Fu's the bureau which remains placidly upright as* JANE *screams with pain.*

ROGER *appears from the kitchen and we notice that there is some smoke coming through.*

ROGER Erm, I don't want to make a fuss but there's erm a smell of er...the dinner...

JANE Roger! Get an axe.

ROGER Er, the cottage pie...

JANE That is not cottage pie, it is hachis au parmentier...

ROGER Yeh, well the hachis...

JANE Roger, an axe.

ROGER Look the...

JANE ROGER!

ROGER Ogh... *(He exits through the kitchen and into the garden)*

PAULINE Jane, let me have a look at your hand.

JANE My hand's fine. Just one blow, one heavy blow.

PAULINE Don't you really think it would be best if we just
forget about...

JANE Never. He might think he's beaten me...

> *The telephone begins to ring and* **PAULINE** *goes to answer
> it.*

> **ROGER** *enters with a huge and heavy sledge hammer.*

ROGER I couldn't find an axe, would this...

JANE Perfect.

PAULINE Jane...no.

> **JANE** *marches to get the hammer.*

JANE Right.

PAULINE *(on the phone)* Hallo, five-oh-oh-nine... Who is it?
*(She looks at the receiver with alarm, begins to scream and
drops it)*

> **JANE,** *who is attempting to lift the hammer turns to*
> **PAULINE.**

Jane...it's *(pointing at the receiver)* It's...the phone. It's...
heavy breathing.

> **JANE** *pushes the hammer at* **ROGER** *and marches to
> the phone.*

JANE Roger. Get that bureau open.,

ROGER But the dinner's... *(He appeals to* **PAULINE***)* Pauline, the cottage pie...

From upstairs there is the sound of a young child calling "Mummy, Mummy".

PAULINE *(calling)* John...it's all right...right, Mummy's coming...

PAULINE *exits upstairs.*

ROGER The dinner...

JANE No, Dennis Cain, you can just stop that stupid breathing now. It doesn't impress me, Cain. *(To* **ROGER***)* Roger. Hit it.

ROGER *(pointing at the bureau)* What the?

JANE Get it open. Now. *(Back on the phone)* We're just about to open this bureau, Dennis Cain...we know what's in there and your game's up. In a second or two it will be open and we will all see the depths to which your mind has sunk.

She sees **ROGER** *tentatively holding the hammer.*

Hit it Roger.

As **JANE** *returns to the telephone,* **ROGER** *reluctantly but obediently raises the hammer above his head.*

You see a psychiatrist and we're going to see to it...

The weight of the hammer above **ROGER**'s *head pulls him backwards so that both hammer and* **ROGER** *land in the centre of the dining table which should collapse.* **ROGER** *scrambles to his feet whilst pointing out of the window, into the garden.*

ROGER Out there...out there, there's someone out there.

JANE Where?

ROGER In the garden, with an aerosol spray...

JANE *retrieves the hammer from the debris of the table and thrusts it into* ROGER's *hands.*

JANE Get them Roger, get out there and show them what you're made of.

ROGER But supposin' it isn't only the Parnes kids...

JANE The hammer...you've got the hammer.

She bundles him out and returns to the phone.

Unseen DENNIS *enters, replaces the aerosols in the bureau and surveys the chaos listening to* JANE.

(on the phone) Now you had better listen to this—a man who makes obscene phone calls to his own wife is obviously very ill indeed and is in need of medical attention... Don't put on that funny voice with me, I know it's you and I also know that you're a pervert, Dennis Cain. We want you to give yourself up without a struggle. That way it would be better for everyone.

DENNIS OK, I surrender.

JANE *double takes* DENNIS *and the phone, screams and drops the receiver. She rushes for the kitchen door and is passed by* ROGER *who enters dragging the hammer behind him.*

ROGER *(to his disappearing wife)* I tried love, God knows I tried. But... *(He turns to* DENNIS*)* Ten of them at least, Den, tryin' to paint your lawn. Overpowered me.

We hear a voice coming from the telephone receiver. DENNIS *goes to it.*

DENNIS Oh, hello Dad.

Smoke is now billowing from the kitchen.

ROGER The dinner. *(He rushes out to the kitchen)*

DENNIS No, Dad, that was not me joking again... No, I didn't mean the supermarket by the chip shop... Dad, Dad, I reckon the best thing you an' me mum can do is invest a quid in fish and chips, fifty p on bus fares an' sod off home right now.

ROGER *enters with a smoking casserole dish.*

ROGER Cottage pie burnt to buggery.

Curtain.

ACT II

*Sometime later the same evening. The Venetian blind
is drawn to cover the window.*

*PAULINE, DENNIS, JANE and ROGER are seated at the
dining table which is profusely littered with empty wine
bottles and aluminium trays from a Chinese take-away
restaurant.* PAULINE *is beginning to tidy away.*

JANE   Pauline, please stop apologizing. It was a wonderful meal.

PAULINE   Yes, but I don't see how I can take the credit for the
cooking at the Chinese take-away.

JANE   And neither can you be expected to take the blame for
guests who can't get here on time and force you to leave a
meal waiting and waiting in the oven.

ROGER   Don't worry chucks, we love Cantonese food, don't we?

JANE   We adore oriental food, Pauline.

ROGER   Food from the East—y' can't beat it. It's subtle on the
palate y' see; none of this English cover-it-all-in-gravy touch.
Canton Cuisine, I love it: Barbecue spare ribs with chow
mein, a portion of curry sauce an' chips—ecstasy.

DENNIS   Me Mum and Dad were in the Chinese chippy.

JANE   When you think about it we're so lucky aren't we? When
you think of the boring food that the last generation had
to put up with and you compare it with what's available to
us—Chinese food, Greek and Italian, Indian food, isn't it
marvellous?

DENNIS   I reckon they must have got hold of an AA Road Map.

JANE It is marvellous isn't it, how we can take advantage of the many different cultures which exist in our country.

DENNIS Me Dad had been in the take-away for half an hour. He had the poor Chinese feller demented, trying to get him to understand how to make spam fritters.

JANE I do think we're richer by being able to absorb from all these other cultures.

DENNIS It was a good thing I arrived when I did; I was just in time to stop me Dad climbin' over the counter to show the poor feller how it was done.

JANE Of course a lot of people try to resist these influences... but not me. You only have to step into our house to see that we willingly take from other cultures.

DENNIS And there's me Mum on the other side of the poor feller trying to teach him how to make real mushy peas.

JANE We often have incense burning in the house don't we Roger? And Roger's got an Indian kaftan dressing gown. There's that African mobile in the hall and the two Malayan tom-tom drums by the chimney breast.

DENNIS It sounds like the headquarters of the United Nations.

PAULINE And you've got that picture of the little Mexican boy, with the tears, haven't you?

JANE Not any more, love. Our artistic taste has moved on a little since then. We've found that's the case with art, haven't we, Roger? You find, you see Pauline, that as you grow more familiar with art, so you can begin to appreciate the deeper forms.

ROGER We gave the little Mexican feller to me Mum. Ogh, she loves him, doesn't she? She sits there for hours just lookin' at him, tears streamin' down her cheeks. She has the time of her life, sittin' there cryin' at the little Mexican lad.

JANE We've got a Lowry on that wall now.

PAULINE An original?

JANE A print of an original, yes.

ROGER He was a primitive y' know. Lowry.

PAULINE Was he Roger?

ROGER Yes, we're very into Lowry now.

JANE I look at that picture and see all those little people streaming out from the mill, dead people, with dead lives, nothing left for them, none of them going anywhere. I look at them and I always think, how lucky we are.

DENNIS Me dad wanted to know who was shriekin' down the phone at him. I told him it was a party line.

JANE When you discover art you open such wide fields for the mind to roam.

DENNIS He said which party was it—the Nazi party?

PAULINE Dennis, I think we've had enough of your parents for one night.

DENNIS And they haven't even been here.

PAULINE What was that you were saying Jane?

JANE It's not only art is it? Just think of all the other things in our lives which make us so much richer than those who went before.

PAULINE I know. I don't know where I'd be without my Tupperware.

DENNIS I think there's something very ominous about Tupperware. How can anyone make a multi-million pound business out of lids that don't fit properly?

PAULINE There's nothing wrong with the lids. It's the people who put them on.

ROGER Tupperware? It's incredible stuff. They were tellin' us, weren't they love, at the convention, about this woman who bought one of their salad storers. One day she goes down to the shops an she buys this big bunch of celery an' she puts it in this salad storer. Anyway, next day, before she could eat it, she dropped dead, suddenly. She lived on her own like an' no one knew she was dead for months an' months. And when they finally broke into her house, do you know what they found? That celery was still as fresh as a daisy. Now that's a recommendation isn't it?

DENNIS What about her family and neighbours?

ROGER Oh, they all got salad storers after that.

DENNIS I hate Tupperware.

PAULINE We've had enough of your pet hates, Dennis.

DENNIS Every time I see a new piece of Tupperware in the house it feels like another little invasion has taken place... It seems to have a will of its own. I dreamt about it the other night. I dreamed that all the Tupperware in the house gelled together into one big plastic mass and began rollin' an slidin' up the stairs, on and on, through the bedroom door and sliding across the carpet, creepin' up onto the bed and pouncin' on me. The more I struggled, the more wrapped up in it I became until finally I stopped struggling and became The Tupperware Man.

JANE They do say, don't they that the most boring thing in the world is another person's dream.

DENNIS An' in the next part of the dream I was Tupperware Man himself—I could fly and everything I touched turned to Tupperware. They sent Superman after me, and Batman and Robin and Luke Skywalker and Wonder Woman. But they were all helpless in the face of Tupperware Man. I turned them all into Tupperware—Batman and Robin became a butter dish an' egg cup, Superman was turned into a picnic box, Luke Skywalker into a salad spinner an' I turned Wonder Woman into a huge, tit-shaped jelly mould. Planet Earth was in danger of becoming a Tupperware Globe when the Americans came up with a new invention—Tupperware

Woman. They sent her after me and I tried to resist, but it was no good, I was helpless in the face of her. An irresistable force drew me towards her, I couldn't stop myself, I struggled to keep away from her but I was drawn on and on. Beaten, I gave up, I kissed her and me lid flew off.

PAULINE I just pray he'll be right after the holiday.

ROGER 'Ey, it won't be long now will it? "We're off to sunny sunny Spain/Vive España". Great, remember it, kid, remember?

DENNIS *(unenthusiatically)* Yeh, I do, Rodge.

ROGER The Fantastic Flamencos at Pepi's Night Spot.

DENNIS Yeh, the Fantastic Flamencos.

ROGER An' the Space Invaders at the hotel. I bet I thrash y' again this year Dennis.

DENNIS Yeh. The space invaders.

ROGER An' Sancho at the beach. He always remembers us doesn't he? He always makes sure we get a spot on the sand. Buenos notches Señor Roger. Never forgets us.

DENNIS Why don't we go somewhere else this year?

PAULINE Dennis, we've booked for Spain.

DENNIS Well let's unbook. Let's go somewhere else else. Let's go to...to... India.

PAULINE Dennis, I don't think you'd like India.

DENNIS But I've never been.

JANE I don't think the Indians are a people I'd like to spend too much time with Dennis.

DENNIS Why? You're always burning incense an' he's got an Indian kaftan dressing gown.

JANE Yes, but that's different.

DENNIS Why is it?

JANE And anyway that was before we saw *Jewel In The Crown*.

DENNIS All right not India. But why not Japan or China. Yeh, China, we could all eat Chinese food till it was comin' out of our ears then.

PAULINE I just know I wouldn't like Chinese food in China. It's different there.

ROGER They don't have curry in Chinese chippies in China, y' know?

PAULINE Anyway Dennis, everyone wants to go to Spain.

DENNIS *(standing)* I don't.

PAULINE Who'd like coffee?

DENNIS Everybody hates Spain.

JANE It is fresh coffee, is it, love?

DENNIS Even the Spaniards hate Spain.

PAULINE Fresh coffee in a bag, yes.

DENNIS That's why the drink's so cheap. You have to be constantly pissed to live there.

JANE That's fine love. I just can't take instant coffee. My stomach reacts against it.

DENNIS You mean it makes you fart?

PAULINE Take no notice of him, Jane.

JANE I quite intend to, my love.

DENNIS And I am not going to Spain.

PAULINE Milk or cream, Jane?

DENNIS I was young once. I was young and free.

JANE Do you have any skimmed milk Pauline? The cholestrol content of milk ordinaire is enormous.

DENNIS And now I am thirty-five. *(He goes up to* JANE *and sticks his face into hers)* Thirty-five, thirty-five years of age.

JANE *(standing)* Roger, will you do something about this please?

ROGER   Eh.

DENNIS   Thirty-five, half-way house.

JANE   ROGER!

DENNIS   *(shouting)* Thirty-five years old today.

JANE   Roger will you do what must be done?

ROGER   Right, right.

DENNIS   Thirty-five, thirty-five, thirty-five...

ROGER   *(with his arms raised)* OK, Kid. OK. *(He sings "HAPPY BIRTHDAY TO YOU")*

During the singing JANE *and* PAULINE *hurriedly exit to the kitchen.* ROGER *grabs a gift-wrapped parcel from the table.*

Here kid, you might as well open this now. It's from Val next door.

DENNIS *rips off the paper with a vengeance to reveal a John Denver album.* ROGER *is beaming over his shoulder.*

Ogh, fabulous kid, fabulous. Now you've got the full Denver collection.

DENNIS, *now maniacal, stares at him.*

Time for a toast eh?

As ROGER *heads for the wine bottle,* DENNIS *grabs the record-carrying case, goes to his record collection and begins to throw Denver records into the case.*

DENNIS *rushes out through the kitchen and the back door.*

So here's to many more thirty-fives after this one kid and may every year be as happy as...

He turns to find himself addressing an empty room. PAULINE *appears at the kitchen doorway.*

PAULINE Roger, what's he doing rushing out into the back with his record-carrying case under his arm?

ROGER Well... Maybe he's testin' it.

> **PAULINE** *exits to the kitchen and* **ROGER** *peers out of the Venetian blinds.*

> He seems to be bendin' down an' doin' somethin'... He's takin' his records out of the carrier... He's er...what's he doin' now? Ogh, he's takin' the discs out of the sleeves... Now what's he doin'? Bloody hell. Would y' believe that? He's glidin' his records... Ogh...look at that one go... Right over the back roof. Ogh it didn't half go that one, look at that one, fabulous, fabulous...

> **JANE** *and* **PAULINE** *enter.*

JANE Roger will you please get out there and bring him in?

ROGER Why? The kid's enjoyin' himself.

JANE ROGER!

> **ROGER** *goes.*

PAULINE Jane, what am I going to do about him?

JANE Just ignore him. Some men do anything to get attention.

PAULINE But surely not Frisbying LP records?

JANE You'd be surprised my love. *(She peeps through the blinds)* Roger...you're supposed to be bringing him in, not helping him.

ROGER *(offstage)* I'm trying to gain his confidence.

> *Whoops of joy are heard offstage.*

PAULINE Will Roger be all right out there? Dennis can be very stubborn you know.

JANE Don't worry about Roger. The Duke Of Edinburgh did not present Roger with his Award for nothing.

PAULINE What am I going to do?

JANE Pauline, it's nothing. What's a nervous breakdown these days?

PAULINE A nervous breakdown?

JANE The doctors will have him sorted out in no time. A little electrical treatment. It could do Dennis a lot of good.

PAULINE I feel sick.

JANE Come on, I think you should have a little lie down. Let Roger deal with this. Now come on, let's wash away those tears. Never lose your composure, Pauline.

They exit as **DENNIS** *and* **ROGER** *enter and head straight for the record rack.*

DENNIS *(pulling out albums)* Neil Diamond.

ROGER *(taking the record)* Neil Diamond. He'll go far.

DENNIS "Wings".

ROGER Ogh, we'll reach the far side of the estate with them.

DENNIS Come on.

The telephone rings. **DENNIS** *answers.*

Hello... It's for you...

ROGER Who the bloody hell...?

DENNIS Baby-sitter. *(He begins to amass more records)*

ROGER *(on the phone)* Hello, Belinda? Yes... Yeah... But there's a fence... OK. Right. Tarrah. I'll be there in two minutes.

DENNIS Right, let's go.

ROGER *(blocking him)* Don't you bloody move an inch.

DENNIS What's up?

ROGER I'll tell you what's up. Belinda the Babyminder was sittin' with the kids, watchin' "Death In A Tumble Drier", on the video when she heard a crash from the garden, followed by another one, and another. Dennis, me you and John Denver have just razed my greenhouse to the ground.

JANE *appears at the kitchen doorway and hears the news.*

ROGER *rushes past her and out.*

DENNIS *watches as* JANE *pours herself a large glass of wine.*

DENNIS Were you insured?

JANE Against John Denver, I doubt it. Right, Dennis, I want the truth. Is it premature ejaculation?

DENNIS *(astounded)* Pardon?

JANE There's nothing to be embarrassed about, Dennis. You mustn't be shy. You must understand that we have to isolate the cause.

DENNIS The cause of what?

JANE The cause of gliding long playing records away, the cause of your refusal to participate on this estate, the cause of you being a somewhat solitary figure, a loner. Why, we ask ourselves, why doesn't Dennis join the weight-watchers, the badminton club, the jogging circle? You're despised because of it, you know, Dennis. Yes, despised. But I say we have to try to understand, to understand even that which we find obnoxious. And to understand we have to isolate the cause. What is the cause Dennis? Why don't you play badminton, why don't you jog? Afraid of showering with the other men afterwards, is that it? Have you got something to hide Dennis, or is your problem the fact that you've got very little to hide?

DENNIS You what?

JANE Is that it Dennis? Do you lie awake at night, fretting, wishing that you had been blessed with larger equipment? Dennis, there's nothing to worry about. You're just a victim of the myth that says bigger is better. Dennis, that is a fallacy. If only you'd read the right literature you'd understand that size, in these matters, is of no consequence. Dennis, I can see that this problem is wrecking your life. You've made it into an enormous problem.

DENNIS I thought it was more of a tiny problem.

JANE You see, Dennis, you turn a serious discussion into something cheap and juvenile.

DENNIS Jane I don't know where you've got this idea that I'm going off my brains because I've got a little dick but the fact of the matter is that I'm very happy with my dick and not having sought the opportunity to compare its size with that of other dicks—I don't know whether it's economy, two star or premium plus and I don't really care because I'm quite content with it but as you seem to know far more than me in these matters and no doubt have a wide range of experience from which to make comparisons perhaps you'd like to pass expert judgment. Here, have a look for yourself.

During the speech, **DENNIS** *has put his hand down his trousers so that he protrudes a finger through his flies. It is this that* **JANE** *sees when she wheels round.*

JANE Put that away. *(Backing away)* Don't bring that near me. You flasher, I was right. Roger. Put it away, put it away.

DENNIS *(calmly)* Jane... Jane.

As she looks he removes his finger and she realizes. He takes her glass from her hand and pours a drink for both of them.

Jane, I don't know where you get the idea that I'm sufferin' from things like premature ejaculation. If I have got a problem...it's got far more to do with going than coming.

JANE Going? Going where?

DENNIS *gives* **JANE** *her glass back.*

Dennis, I think I've had quite enough.

DENNIS Drink it. It might keep you quiet for a minute.

JANE I don't have to put up...

DENNIS I'm gonna tell y' a secret.

JANE Oh.

DENNIS Jane, do you know what's beneath the tiles of the kitchen floor?

JANE *(wide eyed)* What?

DENNIS A tunnel. For the past couple of years I've been secretly trying to tunnel out of Castlehills.

JANE Dennis...

DENNIS No. Listen. I've been slowly, secretly digging for years, trying to tunnel beyond the boundaries, but whenever I finish the tunnel and break through the earth I always look out to find that the bungalows still stretch far beyond me. No matter how far the tunnel goes I never get clear of the boundary. I know there's a world out there—a world beyond Radio Two and Torville and Dean and Richard fucking Clayderman, but I just can't reach it. Y' see, Castlehills is expanding faster than I can tunnel.

JANE *(looking at DENNIS)* Forget it Dennis.

DENNIS I think I'm gonna have to change me tactics. The tunnel won't work. I'm gonna have to walk out of the gate.

JANE Dennis Dennis, you can't walk out of anywhere.

DENNIS I can. It's dead easy. I just pack me things and walk away.

JANE *looks at him, smiles and shakes her head.*

JANE If it was that easy...

DENNIS I can do it, I can.

JANE Then why are you sitting here?

DENNIS What? I'm gonna do it. I am.

JANE When?

DENNIS When? *(Bravely)* Tonight. That's when. Tonight. I'll be off, into the night, down the long and lonesome road.

JANE The A6?

DENNIS The A6, the M6, Route 66, it doesn't matter as long as it's a road.

JANE You won't do it, Dennis.

DENNIS See, if I stay I'll have to give in. Just like you've given in.

JANE And what's that supposed to mean?

DENNIS See, it's true Jane. Look at you. I remember when you were young. God, it's difficult to remember now but, yeh, you were young once and you had dreams like we all did, didn't you? You used to wear faded jeans all the time. Yeh, I remember now. What happened? You had long hair and slim hips and wide wide hopes for the future. I'll bet you don't even remember that do you? But I do. You used to laugh a lot, and joke and sing. Christ, everyone I knew used to fancy you. What happened?

JANE Dennis, I was never like that.

DENNIS You were, you know. You were. Anyway, I've got no more time to talk, I've got to get packed.

DENNIS *exits to the hall.*

JANE I was never like that Dennis Cain. It must be someone else you're thinking of.

DENNIS *comes back with his rucksack.*

DENNIS OK.

Pause.

JANE I was like that, wasn't I?

DENNIS Make up your mind.

JANE I was. There was a time...a time when if I'd looked into the future and seen what I am now I would have...have... But what do you do? What else do you do?

DENNIS You get out. It's dead easy. Look, I'm going. I know I'm going and once I realized that, it was like, like I was eighteen again and the world in front of me was open and available.

ROGER *enters.*

ROGER Not a pane left. Not one pane left. Well, he'll have to pay for it. Tell him he'll have to pay for it.

JANE Tell him yourself.

JANE *exits.*

DENNIS What's up, Rodge? It's only a greenhouse.

ROGER Was Dennis, was. Now listen, kid, I want to talk to you. Your actions are beginnin' to give me cause for concern. You need a talkin' to, lad. I'm going to ask you a few questions, Dennis. And I want you to answer them honestly, right?

DENNIS Go on, go on.

ROGER Now...at this present time kid, do you feel...pretty... pissed off with life around here?

DENNIS However did you guess, Rodge?

ROGER *(nodding)* Yeh, yeh, I can see it. An' y' feel that the life you're livin' is, pretty, how shall we say, empty? Yeh?

DENNIS *nods.*

Mm. An' you sometimes look at younger people an' think, "I wish I was their age".

DENNIS Sometimes. Yeh.

ROGER Mm. I thought so. I'll bet you've even become a little dissatisfied with Pauline, haven't y'?

DENNIS To tell you the truth, Rodge, yeh. I mean it's not that she's...

ROGER No, no...let me, kid, let me. You see, I'll bet I know more about this than you. I'll bet, for example, you've even started to hate people haven't y'?

DENNIS I have.

ROGER Even people close to you, people you love. Dennis, if I'm not mistaken I'll bet you even hate me an' Jane at the moment.

DENNIS Rodge, you wouldn't believe how much I hate you and Jane.

ROGER It's all right, kid, it's all right... I think I would.

DENNIS I don't think you would, Rodge.

ROGER Now look here, kid, if I say I realize how much you hate us, then I do. But I want you to realize right away that hatred like that is perfectly normal. Look, pal, you're not revealing anythin' new to me y' know. Dennis, feelings like those you've just described to me have been felt at one time or another by just about every man on this estate. Dennis, the symptoms you've just described to me are the classic symptoms of humpwish.

DENNIS Hump what?

ROGER Humpwish.

DENNIS What do I do about it?

ROGER Dead easy. Instead of sittin' around wishin', you get out an' start humpin'. A few afternoons off work, spent between the sheets in someone else's bungalow an' you'll be a new man. What you need is an affair.

DENNIS But I don't want an affair.

ROGER Of course you do. There's not a feller I see who doesn't have somethin' on the side. They're all at it on this estate. It's like a rabbit warren. Why do you think there's so much subsidence round here? A feller needs an antidote to his frustration. You know I've got one or two on the go, don't y'? All these clubs an' committees I'm associated with, you don't think it's cause of the good of me health do y'? There's Big Wendy at the Weight Watchers. Pam, y' know Pam at the Tennis Club, been goin' on for some years that has. Glenda, from the Parent/Teachers, Carol from the Ramblers Club, Belinda, the Babyminder. Y' can't beat it, man. Get out there an' put it about.

DENNIS It seems to me there's nowhere left to put it.

ROGER There's plenty more out there, Dennis.

DENNIS But none that I fancy, Rodge.

ROGER Don't be soft, there must be.

DENNIS Well, I suppose... I suppose there is one I've always fancied havin' a crack at.

ROGER Well you get stuck in there an' nip these dangerous feelings in the bud.

DENNIS Yeh, I only realized it tonight but...

ROGER Don't waste a second, get movin' an' get your leg over.

DENNIS Yeh, I've always fancied Jane.

ROGER (*still under his own momentum*) This estate, it's full of... What? What did you say? I am warning you, Cain, here and now I am warning you. That woman is the mother of my children. You keep your distance. Where's your sense of morality?

DENNIS Mine? Don't worry, Rodge. I wouldn't go near Jane.

ROGER An' you better bloody hadn't.

DENNIS Honest. I wouldn't do anything with Jane. I wouldn't touch her.

ROGER What d' y' mean? I'll have you know my wife is a very desirable woman.

DENNIS I know that. But that's not what I want, Rodge. When I was on that slip road today I should have done it. I should have gone, disappeared forever.

ROGER So why didn't y'?

DENNIS I told y'. I had the car with me.

ROGER Well, you could've dumped the car. Left it.

DENNIS I thought of that. But the weekend shoppin' was in the boot. I mean, I couldn't leave those left behind to starve, could I? I know now though Rodge, I know there's no other way out. I can see that clearly, after tonight. I'm not a domestic pet, Rodge. I'm not like you and the rest of them round here. I'm a wild beast, not a cat who's had his bollocks trimmed. I'm a roamer Rodge, Bob Dylan speaks plainly to me. I'm a wanderer and a gypsy and a poet.

ROGER A poet? You?

DENNIS Yeh, me. *(He hands* **ROGER** *a cigarette packet)* Read that.

ROGER *(reading)* Government Health Warning. Smoking Can...

DENNIS *turns the packet over for him.*

In the land of proud vasectomies
Where cholesterol's more talked of than weather
They've Black and Deckered their hopes
Deep frozen their dreams forever.
In the country of Mothercare Angels
Where Tupperware rules OK
They're counting the special offers
They harvested through the day.
In a place called "dead forever"
On the banks of a man-made mere
The only song the natives sing
Is "Christ Get Me Out Of Here".

Not bad kid...not bad...

DENNIS I'm goin', Rodge.

ROGER Goin'? Goin' where?

DENNIS Away, off into the night. Just me, a lone figure at the side of the road, an outline in the truckers' lights, the traveller, the outsider, the one who had the courage to do it.

ROGER Come off it. You're not goin' anywhere an' you know it.

DENNIS You won't say that when I'm gone.

ROGER Gone? Don't be soft. Even if you were serious and you did go, have you thought what it would be like? Eh? What would you be doin' eh? While we'd be here sleepin' under warm continental quilts, you'd be out there kippin' in the grass or on the sand. While we'd be at good tables, eating good food, you'd be sittin' round some bloody camp fire. While we'd be comin' home every night to the same wife an' the same house there wouldn't be the same security for you. You wouldn't have responsibilities. Life would just be an endless list of different places an' new encounters an' fresh women. *(He stares, thinking, then sighs longingly)* Christ, you lucky bugger.

DENNIS *laughs.*

ROGER *heads for the kitchen to find more wine. He closes the door behind him.*

JANE *enters from the hall door.*

JANE Dennis. Take me with you.

DENNIS *(turning from packing his rucksack)* Now Jane... Jane, just hold on, Jane.

JANE You're right Dennis, you've made me realize...

DENNIS Jane...be careful.

JANE I've had enough of being careful. I'm sick of being careful. You're right and I'm coming with you.

DENNIS Jane, you can't. You've got two lovely kids and the most up-to-date fitted kitchen on the estate, now why jeopardize...

JANE Sod my kitchen. Let him have it. The two of us. You and me on the road. Dennis, I'm going to get changed. I'm going to borrow a pair of your jeans.

She exits through the hall door.

DENNIS Jane... Jane...come back it's... Oh shit.

PAULINE, *dressed in anorak and jeans enters from the hall.*

Oh shit.

PAULINE Dennis, we're going away. I've decided that what you need is a rest. There's no point in waiting for a holiday. You could be in an institution before then. No, we'll get away now. To the Lake District. Plenty of walking and fresh air is much better than pills or electrical treatment for a man in your condition. We can lift John into the car. I've packed a few things and we can...

DENNIS *(shrieking)* No, no, no, no!

PAULINE Dennis, don't shout. I know you're not well but at least have some consideration for...

DENNIS I am not going anywhere in the car. I am going on the road. *(He raises his thumb)*

PAULINE Hitch-hiking? Oh that'll be fine won't it? And supposing we don't get a lift?

DENNIS Not we, me. I am not going to the Lake District. I am not going to Spain. I am going to the slip road and going to wherever the lifts happen to take me. Apart from Spain that is. If I'm unlucky enough to pick up a truck going to Spain I'll just get off at France.

PAULINE Dennis. Is this really what you feel you must do?

DENNIS Yes. Yes.

10

PAULINE *(considering)* All right Dennis. If that's what you feel you must do then that's what we'll do. If your health depends on...

DENNIS Pauline, I am not talking about a week, a couple of weeks, a month. I want to go for good.

PAULINE What?

DENNIS Forever?

PAULINE Leaving everything we've built up?

DENNIS Yes, yes. You can have it all.

PAULINE What do you mean?

DENNIS I mean I'm going alone. OK. There I've said it. I am going alone.

PAULINE Oh no you're not. Not in the state you're in. I'm coming with you.

DENNIS How can you? What about John?

PAULINE He'll have to come with us won't he? I suppose other families have had to do it, in the past.

DENNIS Look, Pauline, listen. I'm talking about going on the road, forever—a wanderer, a freak of the highway. It's rough out there. It's hard an' it's heavy an' it's lawless. Pauline have you seen the M6?

PAULINE Yes, and that's why you need me to look after you.

DENNIS Pauline, I'm not a domestic pet.

PAULINE Now there's a couple of pints of milk in the fridge. We might as well take a flask with us. *(She goes into the kitchen)*

DENNIS No... No...

He goes to follow her but is stopped by the appearance of **ROGER**, *well pissed, clutching a half finished bottle of wine and wearing anorak and wellingtons.*

ROGER Kid... I'm coming with y'.

PAULINE *enters from the kitchen, clutching a flask.*

JANE *enters wearing a pair of* DENNIS*'s jeans.*

PAULINE Come on, Dennis.

JANE Dennis, let's go.

DENNIS *looks at the three of them before sinking on to the settee. The three of them see each other.*

PAULINE What's going on?

ROGER What are you doin' in Dennis's trousers?

JANE *(defiantly)* I'm going away with Dennis.

ROGER You're not. Dennis is comin' away with me.

PAULINE Dennis, will you please tell these people that you are coming away with your wife and your child?

ROGER He's comin' with me.

JANE Come on, Dennis. I'm ready.

DENNIS *(sighing)* I'll tell you what—you lot go an' I'll stay here. What's the point anyway? It seems everyone's goin'. Right this minute you probably can't get on to the slip road for the queues of hitch-hikers.

ROGER You? Goin' away with Dennis? You can't go anywhere. You've got your children to look after.

JANE You look after them.

ROGER Me? Me, how the hell can I look after them? I hardly know them.

JANE Yes. You look after them. You try living your life with two kids in a flea-sized dormer bungalow. You try it, because I won't be here. I'm going away with Dennis. Go on Roger... fuck off.

PAULINE ⎫
ROGER ⎬ *(together)* Jane!

JANE What's wrong? Can't you cope with a little real language, a little salty word or two. That's how he *(referring to* DENNIS*)* talks. He understands. He's real.

DENNIS Oh, buggery.

JANE Yes, Dennis, that's it. Real language. Me and Dennis, we're going out on the road. I've had enough of the rest of you. But I don't have to put up with it anymore, I don't have to pretend anymore, look... I'm on my own...I'm wild...I'm free. I'll tell them...all of them... *(She rushes to the window, half pulls up the blind and begins to shriek out of the open window)* Fuck, fuck, fuck, fuck, fuck, fuck... Can you hear me, Val? Fuck, fuck, fuck...

ROGER *tries to wrestle* JANE *away from the window but with a perfectly aimed elbow she downs him.*

Get off me. Get off.

ROGER You can't do this. What about me?

JANE You? You. You can get one of your other little Phase Two wives to look after you.

ROGER What, love?

JANE What love? Do you think I'm blind? I know Roger. I've known for ages, about all of them, all the other women.

ROGER All of them?

JANE Pam at the Tennis Club... Glenda from the PTA... Carol from the Ramblers...

DENNIS Wendy from the Weight Watchers.

JANE Yes, yes, yes.

ROGER Bloody hell. *(Trying it)* Alison from the Swimmin' Club?

JANE I know about them all, Roger.

ROGER An' it doesn't matter?

JANE None of them matter, Roger...because you don't matter.

ROGER Oh. (*Pause. Suddenly*) What about Mavis at work?

JANE Tch. And Val from next door?

DENNIS Val? Bloody hell?

ROGER Belinda? Dianne?

JANE Yes, yes.

ROGER Tracey?

JANE (*bored*) Yes.

ROGER Susan...

JANE From, the supermarket, yes, yes, yes.

PAULINE (*who has been comforting* **ROGER**; *suddenly*) And Pauline, from The Haven. Tell them Roger... Yes me... Pauline.

> **DENNIS** *turns in slow amazement.* **JANE** *takes a step forward.*

JANE (*horrified*) Pardon?

DENNIS (*in disbelief*) You? And him?

PAULINE Yes! Me and Roger. Me and boring old Roger?

ROGER Boring?

PAULINE Yes. A lot of the time. But never on Wednesday afternoons. On Wednesday afternoon it's good. It's very good, isn't it Roger? Because Roger can be very imaginative...

DENNIS Oh, spare us the details...

PAULINE He's so imaginative that on Wednesday afternoons he's not Roger. Tell them, Roger, tell them who you are on Wednesday afternoons...tell them who you are for me...

ROGER (*sheepishly*) John Denver.

DENNIS Ogh...this is disgustin'.

PAULINE Tell them who I am, Roger.

ROGER No...no.

PAULINE On Wednesday afternoons, I am Joan Bakewell.

JANE (*moving towards* ROGER) I'll kill you... You bastard... I am Joan Bakewell...

ROGER Oh, love, I'm sorry... I tried to persuade her to be someone else but she wouldn't. She had a try at bein' Selina Scott but it didn't work for us.

JANE (*in tears*) I am Joan Bakewell.

PAULINE (*jubilantly*) No... I am. And I am wonderful as Joan Bakewell... I am glorious... Tell her Roger, go on, tell her what I am on Wednesday afternoons. Tell her...

ROGER (*with a hopeless gesture*) She's my...my Bakewell tart.

> JANE *suddenly shrieks and goes into a karate stance.* PAULINE *moves to protect* ROGER. DENNIS *slowly begins to smile and then to laugh until it becomes uncontrollable, convulsive.* JANE *tries to lay one on* ROGER *who manages to keep avoiding the aimed blows. Finally* ROGER *and* PAULINE *have their backs against the bureau.* JANE *lets fly with a stunning karate chop and* PAULINE *and* ROGER *fling themselves aside.* JANE *connects with the bureau, the one mammoth blow smashing it into a thousand pieces. Aerosol cans pour forth relentlessly, filling the room. The three of them, stunned, turn and look at* DENNIS.

JANE You?

> DENNIS *leaps on to the settee.*

DENNIS (*wildly maniacally*) Yes, me; me, me. I did it...all of it. (*He arms himself with an aerosol can*) But don't worry... I am going...and going alone... You lot?

ROGER He's mad, he's bloody mad.

DENNIS You lot stay here an' get on with your fornication. I'm not goin' anywhere with any of you. You? If we ended up in the desert you'd organize it; you'd stop the sands from shiftin' an' have the nomads holdin' Tupperware parties... Mad, mad, mad...

He begins spraying the aerosol and scatters them, sending JANE *and* PAULINE *rushing for the cover of the hall and* ROGER *out into the kitchen.*

I'm going...alone... I can do it... I know I can... *(He turns and begins to spray his name on to the Venetian blind)*

JANE *(offstage)* Roger...are you safe?

ROGER I'm in the kitchen.

JANE *(offstage)* Roger...we'll have to bring him under control.

ROGER He's mad, you realize that? He's bloody mad.

JANE I think we all realize that now, Roger... That's why I was pretending to go away with him. He had to be humoured Roger... Now we have to bring him under control.

ROGER He's armed, y' know.

JANE We are aware of that, Roger. But we too can arm ourselves. Arm yourself man, arm yourself... We've got to bring him under control.

ROGER *enters, tentatively wary, hands concealed behind his back.* DENNIS, *who has completed painting his name, wheels, aerosol at the ready.*

DENNIS Move, Rodge. I don't want to but if I have to...

ROGER It's not as simple as that kid. You see I'm armed as well. *(From behind his back he reveals a plastic bottle of washing-up liquid and one of liquid Ajax)*

DENNIS Are you gonna get out of the way or do I have to let you have it?

Unseen by DENNIS, JANE *and* PAULINE *enter from the hall.* JANE *carries a vacuum cleaner tube and* PAULINE *carries the sleeping bag from* **DENNIS**'s *rucksack. They creep up behind him.*

You're not gonna stop me, Rodge, I mean it. None of you are gonna stop me. I'm goin' ...

PAULINE *slips the sleeping bag over his head. It is swiftly pulled down as* **JANE** *binds his arms with the vacuum cleaner tubing.*

JANE We've got him...it's all right...everybody's safe, he's harmless now.

PAULINE Dennis how could you?

ROGER *(moving to the phone)* I'm going to phone the police...

PAULINE No... No... Not, the police...

ROGER Not the police? There's a lot of people round here want the responsible party brought to justice...

JANE *(relieving* **ROGER** *of the telephone)* Roger...you don't mean bringing in the police for Dennis, do you?

ROGER Of course I do.

JANE But Dennis hasn't done anything. Have you Dennis?

There are muffled cries from the sleeping bagged figure on the settee.

Of course you haven't, Dennis. He might think he was responsible, but that's all it is, thought, mistaken thought. How could Dennis have committed these recent outrages? He's one of us Roger...for all his little failings he's one of us and will be seen as one of us. If Dennis was seen to commit crimes in the community then those crimes would, I'm sad to say, reflect upon us, all of us.

ROGER Oh.

DENNIS *(muffled)* It was me. I did it.

JANE Of course you didn't, Dennis, you're deluding yourself. Dennis, you couldn't have done it...because we wouldn't believe you.

ROGER *(pointing at the venetian blind)* What about that?

In one pull of a cord JANE *reverses the blind thereby eliminating* DENNIS*'s name.*

JANE What? I can't see anything.

PAULINE So what are we going to do Jane?

JANE What we are going to do, Pauline, is understand. Dennis wants to go away. Well, perhaps he's right. Perhaps we are, all of us, a little tired of doing what is expected all the time. But, you see Dennis's problem is that he doesn't understand how to organise these things. It's simple really, with a little planning. We've all got a month's holiday haven't we? So, why don't we go on the road?

ROGER Hitch-hiking?

JANE Roger! We buy a truck no...not a truck...an old bus...and we fix it up...

ROGER Brilliant, an' all go away in it?

Throughout the following, and as their enthusiasm for the venture builds we hear increased groans of dismay from the sleeping bag.

Throughout the following DENNIS *manages to get up and, unseen by the others, gets himself out of the door.*

PAULINE We fix it up as a holiday home.

JANE Exactly.

PAULINE Oh, it could be lovely.

ROGER It's a great idea.

JANE We drop out...for a month.

ROGER All of us...in our own bus.

JANE Why not? After all we're almost one big happy family aren't we?

PAULINE Oh, Jane. *(She laughs)* Surely you don't think... I mean you do realize that what I said about Roger and me was just a ploy...to bring Dennis out into the open. I was pretending...like you were pretending...wasn't I Roger?

ROGER Of course you were...

JANE Pauline...of course I realized. The idea of you having an affair. *(She laughs)*

ROGER So we club together, buy an' old bus, right? It could be fantastic y' know. We could do what we wanted with it... put a cooker in...an' a fridge...

PAULINE We could get a portable telly and partition a bit off for the children.

ROGER Anything, kidder, we could even pick up a second-hand dishwasher... We could stop where we wanted...

PAULINE Go wherever we wanted, like gypsies.

JANE Organized gypsies, Pauline.

ROGER It's a wonderful idea. What do you think Den... *(He turns and sees that DENNIS is no longer there)*

PAULINE *rushes to the hall.*

PAULINE Dennis... Dennis... Dennis.

JANE *(to the kitchen)* Dennis... Dennis.

PAULINE He's gone...he's gone...

ROGER He's gone. He's bloody done it.

JANE Roger, the slip road, quickly.

They rush out towards the front door.

As they exit DENNIS *enters from the kitchen, pulling the sleeping bag off his head.*

DENNIS *surveys the empty room, noticing the open front door. He stands, trying to will himself through it.*

JANE *rushes in, heading for the telephone.*

She stops when she sees DENNIS. *She stands for a moment, watching him confronting the door. She holds the hall door wide open for him.*

JANE Go on Dennis, go on. There's nothing stopping you.

She finally closes the door as it becomes obvious that he is not going to go. She goes to the kitchen and reappears with a can of lager. She opens it and hands it to him.

Why not Dennis?

DENNIS *(shrugging)* I dunno. I just can't.

Pause.

Maybe...maybe I'll have another go next year...and the year after that and the year after... Or maybe I'll just... *(He considers)* What do you do on Wednesday afternoons Jane?

JANE Not a lot. Why?

DENNIS Fancy a visitor?

JANE Who?

DENNIS Me.

JANE All right.

DENNIS What time?

ROGER *(offstage)* He's here, Pauline, he's back.

JANE Two o'clock.

JANE *exits through the kitchen.*

DENNIS *absently switches on the TV. We hear a band singing "I SHALL BE RELEASED" (from the album "LAST WALTZ").*

PAULINE *enters, out of breath. She stands looking at* **DENNIS** *as he looks at the TV.*

PAULINE Dennis. I thought you'd gone.

DENNIS Me? I'm not going anywhere.

She rushes to him and embraces him.

Go on.

PAULINE You sit down and watch the telly while I get this mess sorted out.

She begins tidying the room as **DENNIS** *sits in front of the TV, sipping his lager, and listening to the band singing: "ANY DAY NOW/ANY WAY NOW/ I SHALL BE RELEASED".*

Curtain.

FURNITURE AND PROPERTY LIST

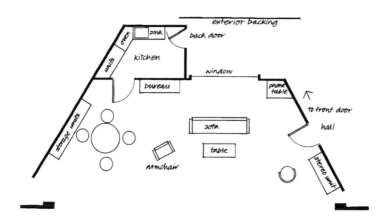

ACT I

On stage: Telephone table. *On it:* telephone
Dining table
4 dining chairs
Armchair
Swivel chair on castors
Sofa
Coffee table. *On it:* 2 ashtrays
Shelves with cupboard units below. *On shelves:*
  books, ornaments
Stereo unit with headphones. *Beside it:* record rack
  with records as specified on page 1
Reproduction bureau with a drop-down flap that
  locks. *Inside flap:* set of table mats, several cans
  of aerosol paint
TV and video recorder

IN KITCHEN:
Kitchen units with an oven and sink. *On the work
  top:* a tray of glasses, several bottles of red wine
  and cans of lager. *In the oven:* a casserole. *By the
  back door:* a large sledge hammer

Off stage:	2 aerosol cans of paint (1 can is empty) (**Dennis**)
	Bottle of red wine, gift-wrapped record-carrying case containing a John Denver record (**Roger**)
Personal:	**Dennis**: key to the bureau, piece of paper

ACT II

On stage:	As Act I except:
	Dining table. *On it:* several empty red-wine bottles, carry-out trays from a Chinese take-away, forks, knives
	Coffee table. *On it:* gift-wrapped John Denver record, two ashtrays

IN KITCHEN:
Roger: 1 bottle of washing-up liquid, 1 bottle liquid Ajax

Off stage:	Rucksack containing sleeping bag, guitar (**Dennis**)
	Vacuum cleaner tubing (**Pauline**)
Personal:	**Dennis**: cigarette packet with a poem written on the back

LIGHTING PLOT

ACT I

To open: General lighting

No cues

ACT II   Some time later the same evening

To open: Overall effect of artificial lighting

No cues

EFFECTS PLOT

ACT I

"Blue" by Joni Mitchell should be playing while the audience
assemble and fade as the houselights go down

Cue 1   **Dennis** put on a record   (Page 1)
          "Blue" should be heard faintly from the
          headphones

Cue 2   **Pauline**: "Dennis!"   (Page 2)
          Volume on the headphones is suddenly
          raised and then lowered until it can
          only be heard very faintly

Cue 3   **Pauline** turns her back and **Dennis** goes
          to the amplifier   (Page 3)
          Volume on the headphones is suddenly
          raised and then cut

Cue 4   **Dennis**: "There was no before..."   (Page 7)
          Telephone rings

Cue 5   **Dennis**: "...a new sewing machine"   (Page 10)
          Telephone rings

Cue 6   **Dennis** puts on a record   (Page 11)
          "Blue" is played softly from the
          speakers

Cue 7   **Dennis** goes to the stereo and turns up the
          volume   (Page 12)
          Verse from "Last Time I Saw Richard"
          is heard then volume down

Cue 8   **Pauline**: "...a god in their eyes"   (Page 15)
          Telephone rings

Cue 9   **Dennis**: "...you an' me Dad can follow the
          tail lights."   (Page 15)
          Door chime plays a snatch of the
          William Tell overture

VISIT THE SAMUEL FRENCH BOOKSHOP AT THE ROYAL COURT THEATRE

Browse plays and theatre books, get expert advice and enjoy a coffee

Samuel French Bookshop
Royal Court Theatre
Sloane Square
London
SW1W 8AS
020 7565 5024

Shop from thousands of titles on our website

 samuelfrench.co.uk

 samuelfrenchltd

 samuel french uk

Lightning Source UK Ltd.
Milton Keynes UK
UKHW021815301219
356131UK00005B/176/P